VOICES OF CHANGE
A SOUTH OAK CLIFF STORY

Written by

ADDIE M. CRENSHAW

THIS BOOK BELONGS TO

_____

_____

_____

COPYRIGHT © 2025 BY ADDIE M. CRENSHAW

All rights reserved. No part of this publication may be reproduced, distributed, or transmitted in any form or by any means, including photocopying, recording, or other electronic or mechanical methods, without the prior written permission of the publisher, except in the case of brief quotations embodied in critical reviews and certain other noncommercial uses permitted by copyright law.

ISBN Paperback: 979-8-9926554-0-7

ISBN Hardback: 979-8-9926554-1-4

ISBN eBook: 979-8-9926554-2-1

DEDICATED

To the bravery of those who dared to make a difference......

The students, the fabulous four, South Oak Cliff Alumni, Principal Shawn Joseph, Hill Jones, Derrick Battie, Coach Jason Todd, the teacher who knows who she is, Dr. Willie Fred Johnson, Dr. Freddie Haynes, Dr. Michael Hinojosa, the community of South Oak Cliff, Next Generation Action Network, Dominique Alexander, my husband Damon Crenshaw II, and son Damon Crenshaw III, otherwise known as Junebug.

ABOUT THE AUTHOR

Addie M. Crenshaw is a nurse, storyteller, and advocate who believes in the power of young voices to create change. A mother and activist, she shares true stories that inspire kids to stand up for what's right. Voices of Change is especially close to her heart, as it helped shape her family's legacy. When she's not caring for others or writing, she loves spending time with her family and encouraging the next generation of leaders to make a difference.

There once was a school in the city of Dallas. In its hay day it look like a palace.

But years later after wear and tear, it was falling apart in need of repair.

You see, when it was hot outside, it was hot inside.

When it was cold inside, well it was cold outside.

Students rushed into school in the pouring rain.

Only to dodge the leaking ceilings, "Yo, this is insane!"

It's hard to focus when a rat runs across the room.

or even harder when you smell a gas fume.

What else could be wrong? The students wondered. "Just a trace of lead found in your water," an expert blundered.

There were four kids, David, Landon, T and Lizzett. A student force no one should ever forget.

They loved their school, were fed up with all the issues. They challenged the board to walk in their shoes.

But it fell on deaf ears little money was given, to fix the school that felt like a prison.

But there was a teacher who inspired the fabulous four. Taught them how they should settle the score.

With the help of activist Dominque and my dad Damon,

all fear was gone. All was left was saving.

"Omaha," is what they yelled.
In all the halls and rooms,
their voices sailed.

Code to walk out, peacefully protest the school.

Just like Peyton on the field, the play sounded real cool.

I know, I was there, just three years old. They held their signs, my dad filmed as the story unfold.

Night after night, they made the six o'clock news.

Gave the Dallas Superintendent Dr. Hinojosa the blues.

So, off to the school he went to see. How bad South Oak Cliff high could really be.

Finally, the school district had a change of heart. How can anyone learn? Now that's smart.

The school was fixed...

and the student's learned better. Grades were up, attendance high

and the football team, took the pie.

Won the Texas state championship two years in a row!

Moral of the story

Give the people what they need and watch us ALL grow.

And...

Closed mouths don't get fed, what my momma always said.

The End...

www.ingramcontent.com/pod-product-compliance
Lightning Source LLC
Chambersburg PA
CBHW051514110526
44582CB00008B/161